DATE DUE

YOUR LAND
AND
MY LAND
ASIA

We Visit

SOUTH
KOREA

Amie Jane

Leavitt

Mitchell Lane
PUBLISHERS

P.O. Box 196
Hockessin, Delaware 19707

YOUR LAND AND MY LAND
ASIA

Cambodia
China
India
Indonesia
Japan
Malaysia
North Korea
The Philippines
Singapore
South Korea

YOUR LAND
AND
MY LAND
ASIA

We Visit

SOUTH
KOREA

Printing   1   2   3   4   5   6   7   8   9

Asia

Library of Congress Cataloging-in-Publication Data
Leavitt, Amie Jane.
 We visit South Korea / by Amie Jane Leavitt.
      pages cm. — (Your land and my land: Asia)
 Includes bibliographical references and index.
 ISBN 978-1-61228-481-1 (library bound)
 1. Korea (South)—Juvenile literature. I. Title.
 DS907.4.L43 2013
 951.95—dc23
                                                            2013033976
 eBook ISBN: 9781612285368

                                                            PBP

Contents

Asia is the largest continent on Earth. It covers more than 17 million square miles (44 million square kilometers), or about one-third of the earth's land surface. It is also the continent with the highest population. Approximately 60 percent of the world's people live in Asia. Asia is part of the same landmass as Europe and is primarily separated from that western continent by the Ural Mountains in Russia. To the north of Asia is the Arctic Ocean, to the south is the Indian Ocean, and to the east is the Pacific Ocean. Asia is separated from Africa by the Suez Canal and the Red Sea.

Some of the major countries of Asia include China, Russia, India, Saudi Arabia, Indonesia—and South Korea. South Korea is located on the Korean Peninsula in the northeastern corner of Asia. On South Korea's eastern coast is the Sea of Japan. Off the southeastern coast lies the Korea Strait, which separates South Korea from Japan. On the west coast, the Yellow Sea separates South Korea from China. On South Korea's northern border is the country of North Korea. For most of their history, North and South Korea were one country. Many people hope that they will be rejoined sometime in the future.

Mungyeong Saejae Provincial Park is one of the favorite destinations for Koreans to visit. Located in the central part of the country, it is known for colorful fall foliage and cherry blossoms in the spring.

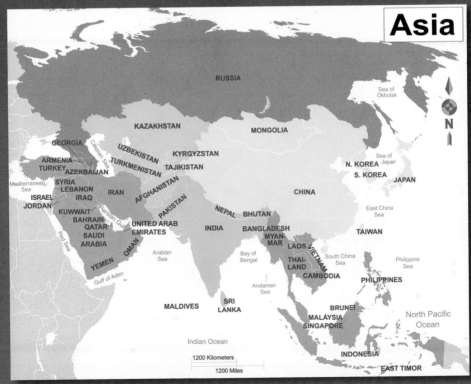

In South Korea, young children practice writing in calligraphy, a very beautiful style of writing that has been in common use for centuries.

Growing Up in South Korea

The sun hasn't yet risen over the mist-covered hills of the eastern horizon, but the alarm clock on the small table next to your bed starts to beep, beep, beep. You roll over to hit the snooze button, then remember that you can't go back to sleep. You must hurry and get ready for school. You have a long day ahead of you.

After you pull on your school uniform, you walk out into the hallway and see your grandmother, your *halmeoni*, preparing your breakfast. Your mother and father have already left for work. They took the train to their offices in downtown Seoul, South Korea's capital and largest city. You sit next to your older brother at the table, where your *halmeoni* has placed a pair of silver chopsticks next to a steaming hot bowl of soup and rice. In the middle of the table, she has arranged small bowls of side dishes: spicy kimchi, seasoned beansprouts, steamed eggs, baked fish, and spinach. Many of these are leftovers from last night's dinner, which is what a traditional breakfast in Korea is like. And your *halmeoni* always cooks in the traditional Korean way. Always.

You finish breakfast, grab your book bag, say goodbye to your *halmeoni*, and walk with your brother to the bus station. You get off the bus first, since

FYI FACT:

A traditional Korean meal always includes kimchi. It is mainly made with cabbage and chili powder, and is fermented in jars over a long period of time.

Korean families enjoy spending meal time together. Most meals feature a wide variety of foods.

you're still in a nearby elementary school. Your brother has to go a little farther, to the high school at the other end of your neighborhood. You say goodbye to him and walk into the school.

Inside your classroom, you have a few minutes to chat with your friends before the morning bell rings at 9:00. Most of the time, you talk about your favorite video games or K-pop group. When the bell rings, all attention must be at the front of the room. That's when the teacher rolls through the door. Rolls? Yes. Your teacher is a robot. Instead of two legs to move from place to place, "she" has a set of wheels.

More than 30,000 teachers are brought into Korea every year from other countries to teach English. However, that is still not enough teachers for the large number of students in South Korea. So the country introduced robo-teachers in 2010.

At first, you and your classmates thought it was a little strange. But now, you're used to it and it feels almost like having a human teacher. The robot is programmed to recognize voices. When someone in the class speaks, "she" answers back and addresses the person by

FYI FACT:

If these brightly colored robot teachers with artificial intelligence prove popular enough among students, they just might replace human English teachers altogether.

name. The only thing you don't really like is that the robot teacher can send reports through e-mail or text messaging immediately to your parents if you are not behaving properly. No one in the class wants that to happen, so everyone is always on their best behavior.

You only have a robot as a teacher for your English class, though, and human teachers for all of your other classes. You split the rest of the morning between math and science classes. Around noon you go to lunch. It's your week to work in the cafeteria, so you help serve the food in the lunch line. Today the cooks made bean paste soup, cooked rice, kimchi, and eggs. Rice and kimchi are served at every meal, so you know they will be on the menu for dinner tonight, too!

After lunch, your class meets in the gymnasium for physical education. Half an hour later, it's back to your desk and your books. You learn about Korean history and culture in social studies and about traditional music, instruments, and art in your music and art classes.

School gets out around 2:00. But you're not done for the day. You catch the bus to your tutoring school, where you spend a couple of hours practicing English. Korean is your primary language, but learning English is important. Everyone knows that English is essential for jobs in international business. That's the field that your mom and dad work in, and you can picture yourself working in a similar job as well.

After English class, you walk around the corner to your taekwondo studio, which is called a *dojo*. Your class starts at 4:30. You started taking lessons a couple of years ago and you really look forward to this part of the day! In the locker room, you change into your taekwondo uniform of white pants and wraparound shirt. Then you join the rest of the students on the mats. After your instructor reviews some basic drills, you spend the next hour practicing your stances, kicks, and punches.[1]

Once class is over and the instructor gives you permission to leave, you hurry back to the locker room to change. You have violin lessons at 6:00 and you must take the bus to get there. Your violin teacher is pleased with your progress on the piece he assigned last week. After your hour-long lesson is finished, he gives you a new assignment and you hurry back to the bus stop to catch your ride home.

You are home by 7:30. Your mom and dad are there, too, but not your older brother. Since he is in high school, he has to go to a *hagwon* after school for intensive studying. Most graduating high school students move on to a university. Each year, that amounts to around 700,000 students.[2] They have to take an eight-hour test to determine which university they can attend. The higher the score on the test, the more prestigious the university they can attend. "There is a narrow gate to the upper schools," says South Korean Kim Hyun-soo. "Because of that, all students are under a lot of school or exam-related stress."[3] That's why your brother spends so much of his time studying. He probably won't even get home until after 11:00, long after you've gone to sleep. During weekdays, you usually only see your brother in the morning—if he hasn't already left for school by the time you get up for breakfast.

So it's just you, your parents, and your grandmother for dinner. Your father cooked tonight. He made his famous kimchi jjigae soup. It's one of your favorites. Of course, you also have some rice with it, too. In South Korea, a meal just isn't a meal without rice. While you eat, your parents ask you to tell them about your day. They want to know what you learned in school and how your after-school lessons

FYI FACT:

Hagwons are after-school private academies for high school students. Because government leaders are concerned that teens are overworked, they limit the hours that *hagwons* can stay open. The current limit is 10:00 p.m.

Kyung Hee University was established in 1949 and serves more than 30,000 students. It received the UNESCO Prize for Peace Education in 1993. The campus is especially beautiful in spring with the blossoming of hundreds of cherry trees.

went. You tell them about some funny things that the robot teacher did today and everyone laughs together.

After dinner, it's time for homework. Your dad helps you with some of your math and your mom looks over your English papers once you've finished them. When they are satisfied, they tell you to get ready for bed. You ask if you can play 15 minutes of your favorite online video game. They agree, but set a little timer by the computer to ring once the time is up.

At 10:00, with your teeth brushed and your pajamas on, you climb into bed. You set your alarm clock. Before long, you know that it'll be beep, beep, beeping. You must get to sleep quickly so you will be well-rested. Tomorrow is sure to be just as busy as today.

Where in the World

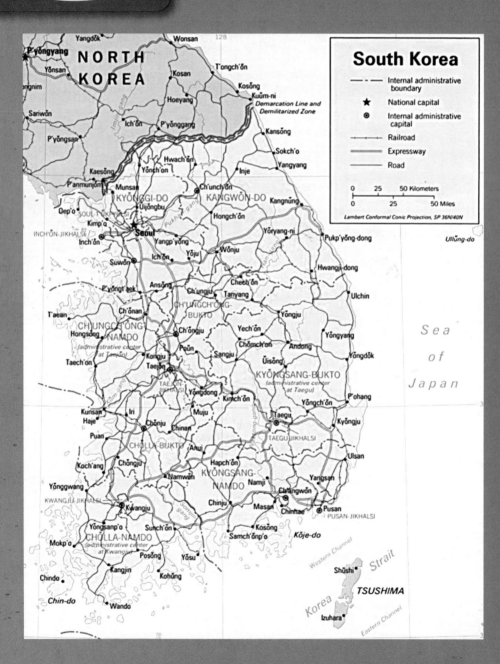

SOUTH KOREA FACTS AT A GLANCE

Official Country Name: Republic of South Korea
Official Language: Korean
Population: 48,860,500 (July 2012 est.)
Land Area: 37,421 square miles (96,920 square kilometers); slightly larger than state of Indiana
Capital: Seoul
Government: Republic
Ethnic Makeup: homogeneous (except for about 20,000 Chinese)
Religions: Christian 31.6% (Protestant 24%, Roman Catholic 7.6%), Buddhist 24.2%, other or unknown 0.9%, none 43.3% (2010 survey)
Exports: semiconductors, wireless telecommunications equipment, motor vehicles, computers, steel, ships, petrochemicals
Imports: machinery, electronics and electronic equipment, oil, steel, transport equipment, organic chemicals, plastics
Crops: rice, root crops, barley, vegetables, fruit; cattle, pigs, chickens, milk, eggs; fish
Average Temperatures: Seoul: August 91°F (33°C); January 32°F (0°C)
Average Rainfall: Seoul: 49.5 inches (125.8 cm)
Highest Point: Halla-san — 6,398 feet (1,950 meters)
Longest River: Nakdong River — 326 miles (525 kilometers)
Flag: In Korean, the national flag is called the Taegukki. It has a solid white background that represents peace and purity. In the center is a red-blue symbol called yin-yang that is considered the country's national symbol. It represents the forces pulling against each other in life and in nature. The symbols in the corners of the flag represent geon (heaven), gon (earth), gam (water), and ri (fire).
National Sport: taekwondo (martial art). Some are also saying that Starcraft (video game) is becoming a national e-sport.
National Flower: rose of sharon
National Bird: Korean magpie
National Tree: pine

Source: CIA World Factbook: South Korea
https://www.cia.gov/library/publications/the-world-factbook/geos/ks.html

Seoul is a very busy place with its bright lights, billboards, and people moving about all day and all night. It reminds many a visitor of another "city that never sleeps," New York City.

We Are Koreans!

Welcome to South Korea!

South Korea is a fascinating country with beautiful scenery, a rich culture, and a long history. Modern South Korea is often defined as "dynamic" and "energetic." That's because South Koreans are always on the go, trying to cram as much as they possibly can into each 24-hour period of time. The phrase "pali pali" is popular in South Korea. Its meaning of "quick quick" definitely describes the people and culture, especially in urban areas. In big cities like Seoul, people talk fast, work fast, walk fast, drive fast, eat fast, and pretty much do everything in their lives as fast as they can.

The majority of South Koreans live in big cities, 83 percent, in fact. Seoul is the biggest city with nearly 10 million people. The next closest city in population is Busan (also known as Pusan) with 3.5 million residents. Most people in big cities live in high-rise apartment buildings. Many of these structures soar 40 stories or even higher into the sky. These big-city apartments can be very expensive, ranging between a half million to six million dollars to buy.[1] In rural areas, people live in single-family houses in small villages which are surrounded by endless seas of green rice paddies, rolling hills, and lush forests. While many people in big cities speak at least some English and possibly other languages in addition to Korean, most people who live in the countryside speak Korean almost entirely.

HanStyle refers to the many unique aspects of Korean culture. The prefix "Han" is used in Korean words such as Hanguk (South Korea), Hanguel (Korean alphabet), Hansik (Korean food), Hanbok (traditional Korean clothing), Hanok (traditional Korean houses), Hanji (traditional Korean paper), and Hanguk Eumak (traditional Korean music).

For centuries, most South Koreans were followers of the Buddhist religion. That is evident by the hundreds of Buddhist temples dotting the South Korean landscape. Yet the number of Christians today in South Korea is greater than the number of Buddhists. In 2013, 31.6 percent of South Koreans were Christian, while 24.2 percent were Buddhist.[2]

In many countries, the population consists of a mixture of people from a variety of nationalities. That is not the case in South Korea. South Korea is considered the most homogeneous nation on earth. That means the country is made up primarily of one ethnic group. Not only do the majority of the people in South Korea share the same nationality and ethnicity, they also share the same culture, language, and traditions.

As a general rule, Koreans are a very respectful people. They bow to each other when they meet, especially to their elders. This bowing isn't anything dramatic like something an actor would do at the end of a theatrical production. Instead, it is just a simple nodding of the head. South Korean Kim Hyun-soo explains more about the respect that Koreans show for each other: "In Korean culture, people are expected to show respect to their elders. So, there are overall two kinds of languages: one is for the elders (honorific or respectful forms) and the other is for people who are the same age or younger."[3]

Family is very important to Koreans. In addition to showing respect to their elders, South Koreans also respect their ancestors. When an elderly family member passes away, the sons and daughters do ancestral rites on the same day. They prepare food for this beloved family

The Seoraksan Buddhist Temple is located in Seoraksan National Park in the eastern part of South Korea. Nearby is the largest seated bronze statue of Buddha in the world. It is 48 feet (14.6 meters) high.

member, and then have a special ceremony. Once they do this, they eat the food in memory of their loved one.[4]

These same rites are repeated for all deceased ancestors on Seollal, the Korean New Year. This is one of the most important holidays of the year in South Korea. The entire family gets together to celebrate. They try to meet at the family home, even if they have to fly, ride busses, trains, or cars to get there. This is the one time of the year that bustling cities can be quiet with nearly vacant streets.

Bowing is a very important part of both Korean and Japanese cultures. It is a way to show respect to another person. Here, South Korean President Lee Myung-bak (left) meets Japanese Prime Minister Taro Aso in Tokyo, Japan, in June of 2009.

The date of Seollal changes every year. That's because it's based on the lunar (moon) calendar. Typically it falls in late January or early February. During this holiday, people generally wear traditional clothing called Hanbok. They eat traditional foods (once again in honor of the ancestors), play games, and give gifts. The main food at Seollal is rice cake soup called *tteokguk*. It's believed that eating a bowl enables one to gain a year in age. After the meal, the younger people bow to the older people and give them a gift. The elders will bestow their blessings on the youth and give them a gift in return, usually money.

The rest of the day is family time. Everyone plays traditional games with each other. Some of the popular games are the board game *yutnori* and the card game *hwatu*. Outdoor games include seesaw and arrow toss. In good weather, families also fly colorful kites together.

Some people will even go on family trips for New Year. They'll travel to historical places in Korea, amusement parks, the beach, or the mountains.

A baby's first birthday is also a cause for family celebrations. Many years ago, babies often didn't live long enough to make it to their first birthday. So when they did, a big celebration was held. This tradition still continues.

This first birthday is called *doljabi*. "Dol" means one in Korean. For this party, the baby is dressed in a colorful *hanbok*. Food is piled high on a table, which is supposed to represent prosperity. The most important part of the party comes at the end. The child is placed on the floor with a variety of objects such as a book, a paintbrush, a judge's gavel, a stethoscope, and even a computer mouse in front of him. The child is encouraged to crawl to the objects. Many people believe that whichever one he picks up first will be his future occupation!

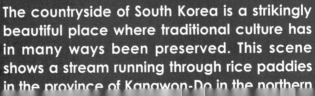

The countryside of South Korea is a strikingly beautiful place where traditional culture has in many ways been preserved. This scene shows a stream running through rice paddies in the province of Kangwon-Do in the northern

Chapter 3

Land of the Morning Calm

Koreans are proud of the fact that they have one of the oldest histories and cultures in the world. On the Korean peninsula, archaeologists have found evidence, such as stone tools and cave dwellings, that date back 40,000 years, or maybe even earlier (North Koreans claim to have found artifacts dating back 600,000 years). Most likely, these early peoples came to the Korean peninsula from present-day Siberia, Mongolia, and China.

Archaeologists believe that these early peoples lived a nomadic lifestyle, traveling from place to place to hunt and gather food. They fished in the oceans and rivers, and hunted in mountains and forests for deer, wild pigs, and oxen. They collected plants such as acorns, turnips, camellia, chestnuts, and arrowroots. Between 6000 BCE and 2000 BCE, these people started settling down and establishing villages. They grew their own crops and raised their own animals. Archaeologists think that the first crop grown by the ancient Koreans was millet and the first domesticated animal was the pig. Between 2000 BCE and 1500 BCE, farmers started growing rice, still the most important source of food in South Korea.

One of the earliest names that Koreans have for their country is Choson (Gojoseon). This name is written with two Chinese characters that mean "dawn" and "fresh or calm." Thus, the English translation for Choson is "Land of the Morning Calm." This name shows that the Chinese had a lot of impact on the early Korean people. The two societies had a great deal of association with each other.[1]

The Cheomseongdae astronomical observatory consists of 365 stones, symbolizing the days of the year.

It's believed that old Choson was a federation of peoples established as early as 2333 BCE. This is when Koreans believe their nation really began. For 22 centuries (2,200 years), Choson stretched across the Korean peninsula and even extended into parts of China. It ruled until Chinese armies overthrew it in 108 BCE. Within a few decades, the old Choson Empire was replaced by three new kingdoms: Koguryo, Paekche, and Silla. The next several centuries were known as the Three Kingdoms period, and Buddhism was introduced to the Korean people during this time.[2]

In 632 CE, the king of the Silla kingdom died. He had no sons, so his daughter Sondok became queen. Queen Sondok reigned for 14 years. She was a very inquisitive person with a quick mind. She wanted her people to advance intellectually, so she sent Korean scholars to Chinese schools. She was very interested in learning about the heavens—the science of astronomy—so she had an observatory built in the Silla capital of Gyeongju. This viewing platform is still in existence today. It is called the "Tower of the Moon and the Stars." It is believed to be the first observatory in the Far East.[3]

In 668, the Korean Peninsula was brought together under one government ruled by the Silla Kingdom. This is considered Korea's first true dynasty. The capital was in the city of Kyongju (Gyeongju), in southeastern Korea. During the Silla Dynasty, over 200 Buddhist temples were built in Korea.

By about 900, the country was broken into three kingdoms again. Then, in 936, Wang Kon—a powerful nobleman—unified the country under the name of Koryo (Goryeo), which is where the name "Korea" comes from. About 300 years later, Koryo was forced to become part of the Mongol Empire.

In 1392, the Yi family took control of the Korean Peninsula and established a new kingdom called Choson (Joseon). Seoul became the capital. One of this kingdom's greatest rulers was Sejong the Great.[4] He became king in 1418 at the age of 22, even though his older brother was supposedly the rightful heir. But people decided that Sejong would make a better ruler. They were right. During his reign, the country experienced many great cultural and intellectual achievements.

At this time, the Korean people did not have an alphabet to represent their language. For centuries, people had just used Chinese characters in their written language. However, this was inadequate because the Korean and Chinese languages were very different from each other. Not all of the sounds and words in Korean could be represented by Chinese characters. This left many people illiterate since learning the Chinese characters was very laborious.

Sejong wanted his people to be able to read and write. So he commissioned a group of professionals to design an alphabet for the Korean language. He wanted it to be easy enough for even the common people to learn. The result was the Hanguel alphabet. It is considered one of the most scientific languages in the world, yet is fairly easy to learn and write. Sejong also encouraged other cultural developments in

King Sejong the Great

science, music, and printing. Because of this, his reign is known as Korea's Golden Era.[5]

During the later centuries of the Choson Kingdom, Korea was sometimes considered a "hermit nation." That meant the country had little communication and association with other nations. However, in the 800s, a geographer from Arabia described the trade network that existed between his region and Korea. In the eleventh century, other writings describe a trade port that was set up in the northern part of the peninsula (now in North Korea). This was a bustling harbor with ships coming in from China, Japan, and Arabia. They traded such things as books, crystals, rhinoceros horns, parrots, gold, silver, rice, ginseng, tiger pelts, paper, and even cow livers.[6]

Contact between Europe and Korea didn't happen until much later, though. There's a story about a Dutch fishing vessel that was

This replica of a turtle ship—the world's first ironclad warship—is one of the featured exhibits in the War Memorial of Korea. Located in Seoul, the museum opened in 1994. Its six indoor exhibition halls and a large outdoor area include more than 13,000 items drawn from the wars the nation has fought.

Characters in the Korean alphabet

shipwrecked on Jeju Island in 1653—some believe these stranded mariners to be the first Europeans to land in Korea. But that isn't the case. The Portuguese actually sailed the waters around South Korea much earlier than this. In fact, around 1543, they established a trading post on the island of Hirado.[7]

About 50 years later, the Japanese launched a series of attacks against Korea. Korea fought back under the leadership of Yi Sun-sin, widely considered one of the greatest naval commanders in world history. Born in Seoul in 1545, he built the kobukson, or turtle ship, which was the first ironclad warship in the world. The entire body of the ship was covered in metal plates—it even had spikes and knives at the top to prevent enemies from boarding the vessel. The front of the ship had the head of a dragon, from which cannons could be fired. Under Yi Sun-sin's leadership, the Koreans won many victories over invading Japanese forces. In one battle, he used his skill to defeat hundreds of Japanese vessels with a fleet of just 13 Korean ships.

Thousands of people witness the ceremonies on August 15, 1948, that marked South Korea's official founding.

The Peninsula Is Split in Two

During Korea's history, the Mongols, the Chinese, and the Japanese all extended their empires into the Korean Peninsula. In 1910, Japan annexed Korea, which brought the Choson Kingdom to an end.[1] When Japan was defeated at the end of World War II in 1945, the Korean Peninsula was split into North Korea and South Korea along the 38th parallel of latitude. The Soviet Union set up a communist government in North Korea. The democratic nations—primarily the United States— tried to help South Korea establish a more democratic system in their country.

South Korea's official name is the Republic of Korea. In Korean, it is "Han'guk." South Korea's "birthday," the day it was officially liberated from Japanese rule, was August 15, 1945. This day, Liberation Day, is celebrated every year in grand style with parades, ceremonies, and festivals.

The first free elections took place on May 10, 1948, and a constitution was written and signed by the country's new leaders on July 17, 1948. Syngman Rhee became the country's first president.

On June 25, 1950, the North Korean army invaded South Korea and quickly seized most of the country. This invasion started the Korean War, which involved not only the two Koreas, but also many United Nations countries (primarily the United States and Britain) on the side of South Korea and the Soviet Union and China aiding the North Koreans. Millions of soldiers and civilians on both sides lost their lives in the fighting.

American troops fire an M20 75mm recoilless rifle during the Korean War.

Even though a "cease-fire" took effect on July 27, 1953, technically the war has never ended since a peace treaty was never signed. The two countries just agreed to quit fighting and stop shooting at each other. Called the Demilitarized Zone (DMZ), the area that divides North Korea and South Korea is still today the most heavily guarded border in the world. Hundreds of thousands of soldiers (including nearly 30,000 Americans) guard this 2.5-mile-wide (4 km) area of land that stretches for nearly 150 miles (240 km) across the entire width of the peninsula from the Sea of Japan to the Yellow Sea. Troops from both sides constantly patrol the area. They are especially concerned about the Military Demarcation Line, which runs through the exact center of the DMZ. Anyone who tries to cross that line will almost certainly be shot.

When it was established, the DMZ didn't just separate the Korean peninsula into two separate areas. It also separated the Korean people. When the "wall" was built between the two countries, families were split up. If you had a brother or sister or a father or mother living in North Korea and you lived in South Korea, too bad. You'd never get to see or talk to them again. You couldn't even call them on the phone or send them letters, either. It's almost like they ceased to exist.

There has always been hope that someday North Korea and South Korea will be one nation. But that hope and desire is fading as the years pass. The people who remember what it was like to have one Korea are fading away with every passing year. Anyone born in the 1950s and later wouldn't even remember what that was like since it didn't occur during their lifetimes. Today, many of South Korea's young people aren't so sure they would even want the two countries to be unified. North Korea has a very poor economy. If it suddenly joined

FYI FACT:

The president of the United States lives in the White House, while the South Korean president lives in the Blue House. The Blue House is actually several buildings, primarily constructed in traditional Korean architectural style.

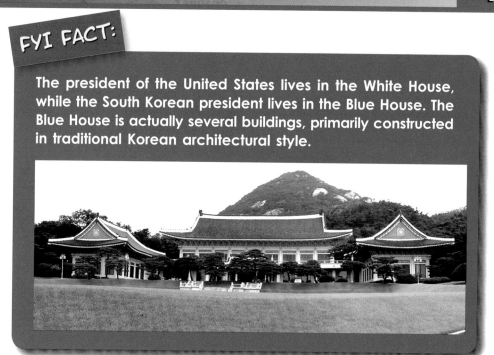

with South Korea, the South Korean economy and people likely would suffer.

After the Korean War, South Korea didn't have free elections until 1987. Syngman Rhee ruled in a very authoritarian manner until 1960. He was replaced by Park Chun-gee, who ruled as a dictator. In 1972, he even changed the constitution so that he could stay president for life. He was in office for 19 years before he was assassinated by one of his aides. Former army general Chun Doo-hwan soon took power in a military coup and ruled for eight years. Still another former general, Roh Tae-woo, became president in 1987 in the first free elections in 40 years.

In December 1997, Kim Dae-jung was elected president. It was the first time in the country's history that an opposition party took over the government peacefully. Born in 1924, for more than 30 years he had been fighting for democratic rights for the people of South Korea. He had been imprisoned many times by previous government leaders because they didn't like what he had to say. He was even sentenced to death. When he was elected, the South Korean economy was struggling. Under his leadership, the country started to do better. He also wanted

Jubilant South Korean relatives hug Go Soon-im (second from left) of North Korea during a temporary family reunion in September 2009. A group of 431 South Koreans were reunited with their North Korean relatives at this time. Some families had been separated for decades.

to improve relations between the two Koreas. In 2000, he held the first meeting with a North Korean leader since the end of the Korean War. They agreed to connect roads and railways between the two countries. They built an industrial center that both countries could share. He even encouraged the North Korean leader to allow reunions of families separated by the DMZ. He called these actions his "Sunshine Policy" because they helped bring light to a once-dark time. Because of his efforts, he was awarded the Nobel Peace Prize in 2000. He served as president of South Korea until 2003.

Because of Kim Dae-jung's efforts, many Korean families were able to be reunited on Liberation Day, August 15, 2000. The meetings between the North and South Korean relatives were monitored by the governments and they could only spend a short amount of time with each other. But the families were still able to see each other again after being separated for 50 years.

Despite his efforts, however, tensions between North and South Korea have not been eliminated. North Korea has been developing a nuclear weapons program for years, even though they signed an agreement not to. This situation remains a continual source of worry among South Koreans. So do incidents such as the sinking of a South Korean patrol vessel by a North Korean torpedo in 2010. Forty-six sailors were killed.

In February 2013, Park Geun-hye became the first woman to be elected president of South Korea. Born in 1952, she is the daughter of the dictator Park Chun-gee. When her mother was assassinated in 1974, many people regarded her as South Korea's first lady. She does not have the same dictator qualities that her father had. She promised in her inauguration address to do everything she could to protect South Korea from North Korea's nuclear program. Through her policy of "trustpolitik," she wants to promote more peaceful communications between the two countries.

South Korean President Park Geun-hye meets with U.S. President Barack Obama at the White House on May 7, 2013.

Looking upward from a meadow with wildflowers toward the summit of Mount Halla. Located on Jeju Island, the mountain is the highest point in South Korea.

Chapter 5

An Emerald Green Landscape

South Korea is a beautiful country with mountains, rolling hills, river basins, low-lying coastal areas, and forests. Mountains and hills make up more than 70 percent of the landscape. There are two main mountain ranges in South Korea. The T'aebaek Mountains stretch from north to south along the east coast, and continue up the peninsula into North Korea. The Sobaek Mountains run down the spine, or middle, of South Korea in a curving pattern that looks almost like a big letter "S." The mountains in South Korea aren't super-high peaks such as those found in other areas of the world. Most of the summits are less than 3,300 feet (1,000 meters) high.

The highest point in South Korea is an extinct volcano named Mount Halla. It is located on South Korea's biggest island, Jeju (Cheju) Island, located due south of the mainland. It rises 6,398 feet (1,950 meters) above sea level. Mount Halla is a national park. At the top of Mount Halla is a large crater that is now a lake. Many interesting landforms called lava tubes are in the area surrounding the mountain. These wide tunnels and caves were formed when lava flowed from Mount Halla many thousands of years ago and then the insides were hollowed out through water erosion.

Jeju is just one of the more than 3,000 islands surrounding the country in the Sea of Japan, Korea Strait, and Yellow Sea. Most are accessible by boat or bridge. Jeju is accessible by air. While more than 500,000 people live on Jeju island, a number of the other islands are

The Yanghwa Bridge is one of numerous spans across the Han River. It is a combination of two bridges. The first one was completed in 1965 and the second one 17 years later. It was renovated in 2010 to allow ships to pass beneath.

uninhabited. Many of these islands are part of the country's national park system. There are a total of 20 national parks in South Korea.

High up in the T'aebaek Mountains, three of the country's major rivers begin as little streams. They are the Han, Kum, and Naktong rivers. They flow down from the mountains into the valleys and empty either into the Yellow Sea to the west of the peninsula or the Korea Strait to the south.

The Han River flows right through the middle of downtown Seoul. It is nearly half a mile wide as it traverses South Korea's capital city. A total of 27 bridges span the Han River in the Seoul area, allowing people to go back and forth between different areas of the city. Walking paths and parks line the river and are magnets for urbanites seeking a break from Seoul's crowds. The city should be called the capital of rivers since five rivers cross through this area. In addition to the Han, the Cheonggyecheon, Jungnangcheon, Yangjaecheon, and Hongjecheon rivers also flow through Seoul.

South Korea has many large lakes, but most are manmade. These reservoirs were formed by the damming of rivers in an effort to conserve water for use by South Korea's large population. Some date back many centuries. Today, these bodies of water are popular recreation spots where people go to play in the water, kayak, boat, swim, fish, and just enjoy nature and relax. Cheongpyeong Lake is east of Seoul and was formed in 1944 by the construction of the Cheongpyeong Dam on the Bukhangang River. Because of an abundant supply of carp in the lake, fishing is one of the most popular activities there. Chungju Lake is the largest reservoir in South Korea, and was created when the Chungju Dam was completed in 1985. Ferries take people across the lake to the various resorts along its edges. Chungju Lake is surrounded by national forests and national parks, which make this area not only popular for water sports but also wilderness activities like hiking, biking, and camping.

Since most of Korea's land is mountainous or hilly, that doesn't leave much land suitable for agriculture. In fact, crops can really only be grown on about 22 percent of the land. As the cities have grown larger in size, less and less land is available for farming. Most of the farmland is in the southwestern and southern plains. Rice, which is grown in wet fields called paddies, is the main crop. Other crops include barley, wheat, corn, soybeans, potatoes, cotton, tobacco, vegetables, fruits, and sweet potatoes. Yet all of these are in relatively small quantities in comparison to the size of South Korea's population. Because of that, much of the food that South Koreans need has to be shipped in from other countries. Fishing, however, is a very important agricultural activity. Waters off the Korean coastlines are considered some of the best fishing areas in the world.[1]

Chungju Lake

South Korea has four distinct seasons: winter, spring, summer, and fall. The states of New York and Pennsylvania have a climate similar to that of South Korea. Winters are cold, especially in the mountainous areas. Temperatures often dip well below 0° F (-18° C). Along the coasts the weather is typically a little warmer. Spring is a beautiful time of the year in South Korea with blooming cherry trees, magnolias, and bright yellow forsythia flowers along the streets and highways. Summer is the hottest time of the year. It's very humid, too, since this is the monsoon season. Monsoon rains begin near the end of June and continue through late July. Typhoons (hurricanes in the west Pacific Ocean) that form near Japan also bring heavy rains to South Korea in the month of August. August is definitely the hottest month of the year, when temperatures can soar as high as 100° F (38° C). That is considerably higher than the average temperature from June to September, which is usually about 68° F (20° C). Autumn is considered one of the most pleasant times of the year in South Korea. The weather is cooler, but not cold. It's also drier, too, since the monsoon season has passed. Leaves on deciduous trees change from deep emerald green to variant shades of pumpkin orange, fire red, and golden yellow. It's a great time of the year to tour the brilliant countryside.

Female Siberian tiger in foliage

Most of South Korea is green. The mountain forests are evergreen jungles with bountiful plant and animal life— approximately 30,000 different species on the entire Korean peninsula. Korea is the home of Asiatic black bears, Oriental white storks, panthers, lynxes, goats, antelope, and leopards. Some of the notable flora include ginkgo trees (among the oldest trees in the world), azaleas, and ginseng root. Unfortunately, some of these species are either now endangered or extinct due to many years of hunting or habitat destruction. One of the most notable is the Korean tiger, now known as the Siberian tiger because it has disappeared from Korea.

Just as the bald eagle is an important symbol for the United States, the tiger is an important symbol for Korea, both in the North and in the South. "People feel very close to the tiger and [they] have personified it throughout history," said Korean artist Cho Hyun-kwon.[2]

According to a Korean creation myth (a story that tells how the world came to be), a tiger and a bear asked the son of the ruler of heaven if they could become human. He agreed. To prove their worthiness, they had to do something in return—stay inside a cave for 100 days and eat only mugwort and garlic. Despite the difficulty, the bear persevered and stayed in the dark cavern for the time required, eating only what was allowed. As a reward, the son made the bear into a beautiful woman. She eventually gave birth to the father of Korea. The tiger, however, just couldn't do it. So he left early, hurrying out in the forest to find something to eat. Ever since, the tiger has been wandering the Korean mountains, slinking through the dense jungles searching for food.[3]

For many years, tigers did freely roam the Korean peninsula, living in the forests and jungles. But not anymore. The last sighting of a tiger in the wild in South Korea was in the early part of the 20th century. Today, the only tigers left in South Korea live in captivity in the Korean National Arboretum. However, it's believed—and hoped—that there still are tigers living in the Demilitarized Zone (DMZ) that separates North and South Korea. A few of the military personnel who patrol the area claim to have seen some through their binoculars.[4]

Visiting Gyeonbok Palace in Seoul is on the Top Ten list for many visitors. Its name means "Greatly Blessed by Heaven." The Japanese destroyed much of the palace during their occupation, though nearly half of the original buildings have been restored.

The Grand Tour

South Korea is a fantastic place to visit because there are many things to see and do. You can visit modern cities, which are some of the most crowded and hip in the world. You can step back in time to old Korea by visiting a Buddhist temple or staying in a country village. You can even spend a relaxing break in nature by hiking in the mountains or forests, soaking in the sunshine on a white sand beach, or swimming in an aqua blue sea.

Here are a few highlights of places to visit in South Korea.

Seoul is one of the most popular cities to visit. This sprawling metropolis is the best example of "dynamic" Korea. It is all bustling energy any time of the day or night. Some people say that New York is the city that never sleeps. This distinction really should go to Seoul. It's not uncommon to be walking through downtown at midnight and see families out with their children, older people exercising in a park, working professionals enjoying a late-night meal, or college students sauntering out of a movie theater.

Seoul is a modern city and an historic one all rolled together. You can see cloud-touching skyscrapers here, yet you can also visit old palaces and temples. A popular place for South Koreans to take out-of-town guests is the Gyeongbokgung Palace, or Northern Palace. It is also called the "Palace of Shining Virtue." This royal residence was once home to the royal family. It was first built in 1395, but destroyed by fire and then rebuilt. Large stone lion statues guard the entrance. The interior features red pillars and a brightly painted ceiling.

FYI FACT:

There are approximately 30,000 dolmens on the Korean continent. Artifacts inside dolmens such as tools and pottery reveal information about ancient Koreans. Many dolmens are protected as UNESCO World Heritage Sites.

Taking the subway is a must in Seoul. It is clean, fast, inexpensive, and reliable. Plus, you can use your smartphone and access the internet while you zip across the city. Cars are a pain here—the streets are just too crowded and there are few places to park. You can also take free shuttle busses between Seoul and other major cities.

For shopping in Seoul, head for Namdaemun Market. The country's oldest and largest market, it dates back to 1414. Koreans like to say that you can find anything under the sun at Namdaemun. Fashion, vintage items, electronics, souvenirs, and even fresh fish are just a few of the things here. It is crowded with vendors and customers on most days, and especially weekends.

Seoul subway

Gyeongju is an ancient capital of Korea during the Silla Dynasty. This city is located in southeastern South Korea and is a beautiful and historical place to visit. You can see the old observatory built by Queen Sondok. You can tour the ancient palaces with their 1,400-year-old manmade ponds. You can walk across ornate wooden bridges and along pine-lined trails towards Buddhist pagodas. Gyeongju also has hundreds of burial tombs. These large earthen mounds are called dolmens and are the final resting place of ancient Koreans. Gyeongju is famous for its bread, a small roll stuffed with a sweet red bean paste.

For adventure lovers, one of the most popular destinations is Mount Seorak. This snow-capped mountain is a UNESCO site, which means it is protected as a nature spot forever. Visitors come here to climb the rugged mountain trails, splash in waterfalls, and see the glorious autumn colors. Hiking to the top of Daecheong Peak (5,603 feet, or 1,708 meters) is glorious, especially to watch the fiery red sun rise above the white-tipped mountain peaks.

In western South Korea on the coast of the Yellow Sea, there are many places with big mud flats which attract hundreds of locals and tourists every year. People like to cover their bodies in the mud and then rinse off in the Yellow Sea. This is supposed to help skin be healthier. A big mud festival is held in the town of Boryeong every July. People put on their swimming suits and run through obstacle courses of mud, jump in swimming pools of mud, slip down mud slides, and splash their friends with mud.

More than 50 Buddhist temples in the South Korean mountains allow visitors. Guests have their own rooms, arranged traditionally with a sleeping mat on the floor and kept warm by floor heaters. Every morning at 4:00, guests are invited to take part in meditation and prayer services at the temple. Throughout the day, guests can hike along mountain trails, help with community service, and eat with the Buddhist monks. One of the rules is that you are welcome to eat as much as you want, but whatever you put on your plate must be consumed. It is considered rude and wasteful to take food and then not eat it. Buddhist monks are vegetarians, so everything served here is made from the various plants that grow in the area.

Seoraksan National Park is one of the first national parks in South Korea. Its 63 square miles (164 square kilometers) have a wide variety of animals and plants. The highest peak is Daecheongbong, at an altitude of 5,604 feet (1,708 meters).

PC bangs are all the rage in South Korea. It's where the party's at for many teens and early twenty-somethings.

Having Fun!

When you ask a South Korean what kinds of games kids like to play, you might expect to hear about playground games or sports. Instead, you'll most likely hear such responses as "StarCraft," "Halo," and "World of Warcraft." In 21st century South Korea, the most popular source of entertainment for many people is the electronic video gaming industry.

South Korea is dubbed the "most wired country in the world," which means that nearly everyone has access to electronics, especially the internet.[1] As of 2013, South Korea has the fastest internet connection anywhere on Earth. South Koreans can access high-speed internet just about anywhere and everywhere: from their phones, from their schools and homes, from their offices, from public gaming spaces called PC bangs, and even from the subway. Because of that—and the overall competitive nature of South Korean culture in general—gaming has become a nationally renowned activity. In fact, electronic gaming is even considered a sport in South Korea, known as electronic-sport or e-sport. People who compete in e-sport are usually young adult professionals who spend their "workday" perfecting their skills in various video games. In other words, these e-sport athletes get paid to play video games all day long, and sometimes long into the night.

Over the past few decades, gaming has become so popular in South Korea that reality television shows have been made about it. Most nights of the week, you can watch professional gamers vie against each other for the top scores. These pros are considered celebrities in South

Korean culture and often make hundreds of thousands of dollars every year in competitions, sponsorships, and salaries. They compete in South Korean competitions as well as e-sport games around the world, including the World Cyber Games, widely considered the Olympics of e-sport.

Most e-sport athletes go by pseudonyms, or fake names. For example, Lee Jung-hoon is one of South Korea's most popular professional gamers. He goes by the pseudonym "MarineKing." Like many e-sport athletes, Jung-hoon was just a young child when he got into gaming. He told CNN reporter John Sutter, "When I played 'StarCraft' for the first time, it was like a fantasy. I felt like I discovered a new joy in my life."[2]

Today, MarineKing is part of Team Prime, an e-sport team that competes throughout South Korea and the world. He lives in a high rise in Seoul with his teammates. Every day, the team spends hours and hours perfecting their strategies in StarCraft and other online games.

Besides video games, what other kinds of activities are popular in South Korean culture?

South Koreans love watching and playing sports. Taekwondo, baseball, golf, swimming, speed skating, figure skating, and archery all make the list of their favorites. Soccer is also popular. K-league is the country's national soccer league. In 2002, Japan and South Korea co-hosted soccer's World Cup, with matches at ten stadiums in each country. South Korea—which is by far the most successful soccer team in Asia, with appearances in nine World Cups—placed fourth, its highest-ever finish.

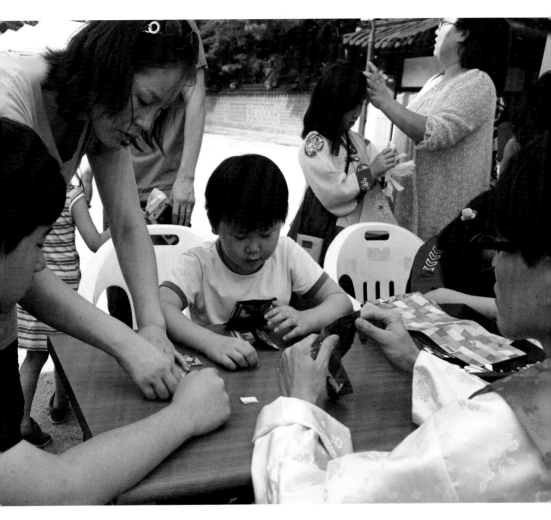

Families in South Korea enjoy touring historical sites and doing activities together. Here they make traditional Korean pouches while on a visit to Woonhyeon-goong Palace in Seoul during the Chuseok holiday. One of the country's two major holidays, it occurs in early fall to give thanks for an abundant harvest.

South Korea hosted the Summer Olympics in 1988, and the 2018 Winter Olympics are scheduled to be held in Pyeongchang. South Korea has won more Olympic gold medals than any other country in archery, short track speed skating, and taekwando. Perhaps the

South Korean athletes compete in a variety of world sports championships. Here, Hwang Young-cho wins the marathon run at the 12th Asian Games in Hiroshima, Japan. Two years earlier, he won the marathon at the Olympic Games in Barcelona, Spain.

country's most famous Olympic champion is Sohn Kee-chung, who won the marathon run at the 1936 Olympics in Berlin, Germany. Because Korea was controlled by Japan at that time, he was forced to compete for Japan and had to change his name to Son Kitei. Sohn was very unhappy with this situation. On the award stand he clutched a small oak tree to cover up the Japanese flag on his sweatshirt and bowed his head in shame. He remained active in running for many years, and coached the second South Korean marathon champion, Hwang Young-cho, in the 1992 Olympics in Barcelona, Spain.

Every October, South Korea holds its week-long National Sports Festival, featuring 39 different sports. In January, a similar event is held for children where young athletes in elementary and middle school can compete in such events as figure skating, ice hockey, skiing, and speed skating.

Many people like to go to the movies in South Korea: both Korean-made films and Hollywood blockbusters are featured on the big screen. When you go to a theater in South Korea, you have the option of buying tickets at a regular movie theater, or you can try out a 4-D IMAX theater. In a 4-D theater, you get to wear glasses so you can see things pop out of the screen just like in a 3-D theater. In addition, the theater is equipped to shoot bursts of air to feel like wind, spray mists of water to feel like rain, vibrate seats to feel like a car's engine or rumbling earthquake, and shower delightful aromas at the appropriate moments in the film. This added dimension provides the full 4-D movie-going experience!

Fine art has always been important in Korean culture. The Insadong district of Seoul is now the country's main art market with numerous galleries that exhibit and sell fine art. Art ranges from painting to pottery and sculpture, most of which have the nature theme which is traditional in Korean art. The most famous galleries are the Hakgojae Gallery and Gana Art Gallery. Every Saturday in this area, the streets are blocked off to vehicle traffic. People can walk along looking at outdoor art booths, listening to musical performances, and dining on such traditional street fare such as Korean taffy and Korean pancakes.

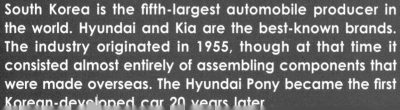

South Korea is the fifth-largest automobile producer in the world. Hyundai and Kia are the best-known brands. The industry originated in 1955, though at that time it consisted almost entirely of assembling components that were made overseas. The Hyundai Pony became the first Korean-developed car 20 years later.

K-Wave: Taking the World by Storm

After the Korean War, South Korea was in shambles. Millions of people of all ages had died, and many cities and towns were severely damaged by gunfire. The economy was struggling with a lack of industries and skilled workers.

History has proven that very little can really get the South Korean people down. They are hardworking, determined, and focused. They put all of those traits to good use after the war and came roaring back with one of the most productive economies in the world. This is known as the "Miracle on the Han River."[1] It is called that because Seoul, the capital of South Korea, is on the Han River and much of the economic advancement has sprung from that area. South Korea leads the world in shipbuilding and has strong electronics, manufacturing, and auto-building industries. South Koreans are also very educated, giving the country a highly skilled workforce.

In the 21st century, there is a "Second Miracle on the Han," or the "K-Wave." This refers to the spread of much of Korea's culture around the globe in music, art, drama, food, language, and culture.[2]

K-pop is the pop music of Korea. Artists from this musical style are rising to the top of international charts. Psy is a prime example. Born in 1977, he discovered his love for music as a teenager and has been a popular artist in Korea since 2001. However, in 2012, his song "Gangnam Style," with its catchy tune and fun video, went viral—the YouTube video was the first in history to get one billion views. People everywhere seemed to be getting their "Gangnam Style" on.

Cheerleaders performed routines to it at football games. Talk show hosts tried to learn the dance style on the air. Unknown artists put together their own video spoofs of the song on YouTube. And Psy performed the song in a mix with MC Hammer at the American Music Awards (AMA) in November 2012. It seemed like if you hadn't heard of Gangnam Style, you simply weren't on this planet.[3] Psy's real name is Park Jae-sang. He said that his stage name is short for psycho. As he told the British Broadcasting Corporation, "In my case, what I thought was: crazy about music, dancing, performers—so that kind of psycho."[3]

Korean food is also becoming the rage around the world. People are realizing that it is not only delicious, but also very healthy.

Dining Korean style is a full-table affair. The main courses come with a wide variety of small side dishes.

Psy and Gangnam Style took the world by storm in 2012. Here Psy (far right) performs at the finals of soccer's Italian Cup in May 2013.

Traditional Korean food tries to incorporate the colors green, white, red, black, and yellow. It also encourages the use of vegetables, beans, and smaller portions of lean meats. The dish BiBimBap is one example of this idea of adding colors and healthy ingredients into one delicious dish. It usually consists of rice, meat, vegetables, chili paste, an egg, and other ingredients.

Korean restaurants are popping up all over the world, even in small towns. People are learning to make Korean food in their homes. You can, too, with the recipe for kimchi jjigae on the next page.

South Koreans have always had their own unique sense of style. Now, their fashions are being featured on runways around the world from Seoul to New York to Milan. In fact, some journalists in 2012 stated that Korean fashion was considered the hottest trend in the world. The prints of South Korean clothing tend to be dramatic and the colors are usually bold. Oftentimes, different types of prints are mixed together in one outfit. Many K-pop artists wear Korean fashion. So when kids see their favorite singers wearing certain clothes, they want to wear them too.

Now that more people around the world have been introduced to Korean culture, it's doubtful that the K-Wave will stop anytime soon. We'll probably see more of our lives influenced by Korean culture in the future. After all, there are many exciting aspects of Korean culture, history, and language that are fun to include in our everyday lives.

The K-Wave is likely here to stay.

Kimchi Jjigae, or kimchi stew, is one of the most popular soups in Korean cooking. It is slightly spicy and sweet and is particularly wonderful if eaten when you have a cold. It is also known to have health benefits because of the kimchi and tofu. This soup beats chicken noodle any day!

Ingredients:
½ pound beef or pork, cubed
3 cups Napa-cabbage kimchi
2 cups water
1 heaping tablespoon gochujang (Korean chili pepper paste)
8 ounces tofu, sliced into rectangles or cubed
½ to 1 teaspoon sugar (optional)
1 tablespoon mirin (optional)
½ to 1 tablespoon canola or grapeseed oil

Directions:
Prepare the following recipe with adult supervision:
1. Place a medium-sized pot on the stove on medium-high heat.
2. Spread the oil on the bottom of the pot.
3. Add the meat.
4. Cook until meat is browned on both sides.
5. Add kimchi, water, gochujang, and sugar (if using).
6. Bring the ingredients to a boil. Then turn down the heat to simmer.
6. Simmer for at least 45 minutes.
7. Continue to cook for 10-15 minutes. Remove the lid part way (or open the vent on the lid). This will allow the stew to thicken. Add more water later if the stew gets too thick.
8. Add tofu and mirin (if using) towards the end of cooking.
   Serve with steamed rice. Garnish with chopped green onions if desired.
Serves 4 people

Korean summers can get very hot and humid. Traditionally, people used paper fans to keep themselves cool. Today, most people have air conditioning, so the fans aren't all that necessary. Yet they're still nice to use on a crowded bus or train or while walking along a busy street.

The Taegeuk is the symbol in the center of the South Korean flag. This symbol dates back many centuries and it is carved into many ancient stones. The Taegeuk usually just has red and blue in it. The Sam Taegeuk has red, blue, and yellow. This symbol was used in the 1988 Olympic Games in Seoul. Red means earth, blue means heaven, and yellow means people.

Materials
- 1 lunch-size paper plate
- pencil
- red, blue, and yellow paints
- paint brush
- glue
- craft stick

Instructions
1. Look at the picture of the Sam Taegeuk. Sketch the "wave" patterns onto the plate with the pencil. It doesn't have to be perfect, just do your best.
2. On an appropriate surface (table covered with newspapers, for example), paint your plate. Paint each wave pattern with the correct color so your Sam Taegeuk looks just like the picture.
3. Let the paint dry completely.
4. Glue the craft stick on the backside of the plate. Leave half of the stick hanging out from the bottom of the Sam Taegeuk to make a handle for your fan.

TIMELINE

Dates BCE

40,000 First people are believed to have arrived on Korean Peninsula.

6000 People begin establishing permanent settlements on Korean Peninsula.

2333 The Old Choson kingdom is established.

108 Chinese armies overthrow Old Choson. The empire is replaced by three kingdoms: Koguryo, Paekche, Silla.

Dates CE

632 Queen Sondok becomes the first woman to rule Korea.

668 Silla Kingdom establishes control over Korean Peninsula.

800s Arab geographers describe their trade network with Korea.

936 Wang Kon unifies the country under the name Koryo (Goryeo). This is where the name Korea originates.

1000s Ports in the northern area of the peninsula (now North Korea) are bustling with trade. Ships come here from as far as Arabia.

ca. 1230 Printing press with metal moveable type is invented.

1377 The Buddhist book *Jikji* becomes the first book published with a printing press using moveable type.

1392 Yi family establishes the new Choson kingdom and Seoul is made the capital.

1418 Sejong the Great becomes the fourth king of Choson.

1543 Portuguese set up trading post on island of Hirado.

1545 Yi Sun-sin, one of the greatest naval commanders in Korean history, is born. He later develops the "turtle ship," considered the world's first ironclad warship.

1653 Dutch merchants are shipwrecked on Jeju Island.

1895 Japan defeats China in the Sino-Japanese War, ending China's influence over the Korean peninsula.

1905 Japan gains control over Korea by winning the Russo-Japanese War.

1910 Japan formally annexes the Korean peninsula and rules it as a colony.

1945 Korea is officially liberated from Japanese rule on August 15 and this day is celebrated annually as Liberation Day; the country is soon divided into North Korea and South Korea along the 38th parallel.

1948 First free elections take place in South Korea. Syngman Rhee is elected president.

1950 North Korean army invades South Korea on June 25, which starts the Korean War.

1953 A cease-fire is agreed to, but no peace treaty is ever signed.

1972 Dictator Park Chun-gee changes the constitution so that he can "reign" as president for life.

1980s Korea focuses more of its economy on high-tech and computer industry.

1987 The Korean constitution is restored to allow free elections of the president.

1988 Seoul hosts the Summer Olympic Games.

1997 Kim Dae-jung is elected president after nearly a lifetime of trying to restore democratic principles to South Korea and begins his "Sunshine Policy" of increased political contact with North Korea.

2000   Kim Dae-jung meets in June with North Korean leader Kim Jong-Il, the first time leaders from the two countries have met since the Korean War. Because of his efforts, Kim Dae-jung is awarded the Nobel Peace Prize. On Liberation Day (August 15), many North and South Korean families who have been separated are reunited for short government-controlled meetings.

2007   Passenger trains are allowed to move across the DMZ between North and South Korea for the first time since before the Korean War. Korean leaders promise to formally discuss an official end to the Korean War.

2008   South Korean historical landmark, the Namdaemun Gate, is destroyed by arson; it is rebuilt five years later.

2013   Park Geun-hye, daughter of Park Chun-gee, is elected the first female president of South Korea.

2014   Korea Republic makes an 8th straight World Cup trip to the Brazil games.

2018   Olympic games to be held in Pyeongchang, South Korea.

CHAPTER NOTES

Chapter 1: Growing Up in South Korea
1.   "2012 Olympics: Taekwondo rule changes," Korea.net, July 26, 2012, http://www.korea.net/NewsFocus/Sports/view?articleId=101520
2.   Jiyeon Lee, "South Korean students' 'year of hell' culminates with exams day," CNN, November 13, 2011. http://www.cnn.com/2011/11/10/world/asia/south-korea-exams
3.   Kim Hyun-soo, personal interview with the author.

Chapter 2: We are Koreans!
1.   Son Seong Jun, personal interview with author.
2.   *CIA World Factbook: South Korea.* https://www.cia.gov/library/publications/the-world-factbook/geos/ks.html
3.   Kim Hyun-soo, personal interview with the author.
4.   Ibid.

Chapter 3: Land of the Morning Calm
1.   Michael J. Seth, *A History of Korea: From Antiquity to the Present* (Plymouth, United Kingdom: Rowman & Littlefield Publishers, Inc., 2011), pp. 10–14.
2.   Se-Woong Koo, "Buddhism to Korea: An Overview," Stanford Program on International And Cross-Cultural Education. http://spice.stanford.edu/docs/introduction_of_buddhism_to_korea_an_overview/
3.   "Queen Sondok (or Sonduk): Silla Dynasty," Women in World History. http://www.womeninworldhistory.com/heroine7.html
4.   Donald Clark, "South Korea," Scholastic. http://www.scholastic.com/teachers/article/south-korea
5.   "King Sejong the Great and the Golden Age of Korea," Asia Society. http://asiasociety.org/countries/traditions/king-sejong-great
6.   Robert Neff, "Jeju featured in early European contact," *The Jeju Weekly*, August 3, 2009. http://www.jejuweekly.com/news/articleView.html?idxno=191
7.   "The Discovery of Korea," Henny Savenjie (ed.), *The Journal of Hamel and Korea* (translated by Jean-Paul Buys). http://www.hendrick-hamel.henny-savenije.pe.kr/holland4.htm

Chapter 4: The Peninsula Is Split in Two
1. Lee Tae-hoon, "1910 Korea-Japan annexation treaty invalid," The Korean Times, August 11, 2010. http://www.koreatimes.co.kr/www/news/ nation/2010/08/116_71250.html

Chapter 5: An Emerald Green Landscape
1. "Agriculture, South Korea," Country Studies.us. http://countrystudies.us/ south-korea/52.htm
2. Gavin Hudson, "Korean Tigers Back from the Brink of Extinction, But Not in South Korea," Ecolocalizer, November 24, 2008. http://ecolocalizer.com/2008/11/24/ korean-tigers-back-from-the-brink-of-extinction-but-not-in-south-korea/
3. Ibid.
4. Euince Yoon, "Tracking Tigers in Korea's DMZ," CNN, May 10, 2010. http://www.cnn.com/2010/TECH/science/05/09/tiger.tracking.dmz/index.html

Chapter 7: Having Fun!
1. "South Korea: The Most Wired Place on Earth," PBS Frontline. http://www.pbs.org/ frontlineworld/stories/south_korea802/
2. John D. Sutter, "Gaming Reality," CNN. http://www.cnn.com/interactive/2012/08/ tech/gaming.series/korea.html

Chapter 8: K-Wave: Taking the World by Storm
1. Jurgen Kleiner, *Korea: A Century of Change* (River Edge, New Jersey: World Scientific Publishing, 2001), p. 254.
2. History Channel: South Korea, a Nation to Watch, Documentary
3. Shawn S. Lealos, "Psy explains what his name means, nears 1 billion YouTube views," examiner.com, December 4, 2012. http://www.examiner.com/article/ psy-explains-what-his-name-means-nears-1-billion-youtube-views

FURTHER READING

Books

Bowler, Ann Martin. *All About Korea: Stories, Songs, Crafts, and More*. North Clarendon, Vermont: Tuttle Publishing, 2011.

Cheung, Hyechong. *K Is for Korea (World Alphabets)*. London: Frances Lincoln Children's Books, 2008.

Mahoney, Judy. *Teach Me Everyday Korean*. Minnetonka, Minn.: Teach Me Tapes, 2008.

Miller, Jennifer. *South Korea* (Country Explorers). Minneapolis, Minn.: Lerner Classroom, 2010.

Walters, Tara. *South Korea* (New True Books: Geography). Danbury, Conn.: Childrens Press, 2008.

On the Internet

"South Korea," Around the World, Time for Kids
    http://www.timeforkids.com/destination/south-korea

"South Korea," National Geographic Kids
    http://kids.nationalgeographic.com/kids/places/find/south-korea/

Official Website of the Republic of Korea
    http://www.korea.net/

Official Korea Tourism Organization
    http://english.visitkorea.or.kr/enu/index.kto

CIA World Factbook: South Korea
https://www.cia.gov/library/publications/the-world-factbook/geos/ks.html

"Han Style," Official Korean Tourism Organization. http://english.visitkorea.or.kr/enu/CU/CU_EN_8_1.jsp

"History," Korea.net. http://www.korea.net/AboutKorea/Korea-at-a-Glance/History

Kandari, O.P. *Tourism, Biodiversity and Sustainable Development*. Delhi, India: Isha Books, 2004.

"King Sejong the Great and the Golden Age of Korea," Asia Society,
http://asiasociety.org/countries/traditions/king-sejong-great

Kleiner, Jurgen. *Korea: A Century of Change*. River Edge, New Jersey: World Scientific Publishing, 2001.

Lee, Jiyeon. "South Korean students' 'year of hell' culminates with exams day," CNN, November 13, 2011. http://www.cnn.com/2011/11/10/world/asia/south-korea-exams

Lee Tae-hoon. "1910 Korea-Japan annexation treaty invalid," *The Korea Times*, August 11, 2010 http://www.koreatimes.co.kr/www/news/nation/2010/08/116_71250.html

Mahr, Krista. "The 50 Best Inventions of 2010: The English-Teaching Robot," *Time*, November 11, 2010 http://www.time.com/time/specials/packages/article/0,28804,2029497_2030615_2029711,00.html

"Movable Type," Princeton University http://www.princeton.edu/~achaney/tmve/wiki100k/docs/Movable_type.html

Neff, Robert. "Jeju featured in early European contact," *The Jeju Weekly*, August 3, 2009. http://www.jejuweekly.com/news/articleView.html?idxno=191

"Queen Sondok (or Sonduk): Silla Dynasty," Women in World History. http://www.womeninworldhistory.com/heroine7.html

Seth, Michael J. *A History of Korea: From Antiquity to the Present*. Plymouth, United Kingdom: Rowman & Littlefield Publishers, Inc., 2011.

Personal Interviews

Kim Hyun-soo (interviewed on February 22, 2013) is a native of South Korea, as were all of his ancestors before him. He grew up and was educated in an urban area of South Korea. He came to the United States as a graduate student. He is an excellent resource on Korean culture, language, history, and geography.

Angela Ahn (interviewed on February 23, 2013) is a second-generation Korean American. Her parents both grew up in South Korea and immigrated to the United States as adults. They raised their three children to appreciate all aspects of their Korean heritage: language, customs, holidays, culture, and history. Angela has been to South Korea many times to visit family members who still live there.

Son Seong Jun (interviewed on February 24, 2013) was born and raised in South Korea, as were all of his ancestors before him. He has lived in both urban and rural areas of South Korea and consequently has an in-depth knowledge of the language, culture, history, and customs of his homeland. He attended graduate school in the United States.

GLOSSARY

ancestors (an-SEHS-turs)—People in your family who come before you: grandparents, great-grandparents, etc.

dojo (DOH-jo)—A studio where taekwondo is taught.

hagwon (HAHG-wahn)—A school of intense studying that high school students attend after regular school hours.

halmeoni (hah-MO-nee)—Grandmother, in Korean.

Hanbok (HAHN-book)—Traditional Korean clothing.

Hanguel (HAHN-gool)—The official Korean alphabet.

Hanguk (HAHN-gook)—South Korea, in Korean.

Hanguk-Eumak (HAHN-gook OO-mack)—Traditional Korean music.

Hanji (HAHN-jee)—Traditional Korean paper.

Hanok (HAHN-ahk)—Traditional Korean houses.

Hansik (HAHN-sick)—Korean cuisine.

HanStyle (HAHN-style)—The overall unique aspects of Korean culture.

homogeneous (hoh-moh-JEE-nee-ous)—Of one nationality.

hwatu (WAH-too)—A card game played on the Korean New Year.

kimchi (KIM-chee)—A traditional Korean dish made primarily with chili powder and cabbage.

kimchi jjigae (KIM-chee GEE-gay)—A traditional Korean stew made with kimchi, meat, and tofu.

metropolitan (meh-troh-PAHL-ih-tuhn)—A large urban area.

pali-pali (PAH-lee-PAH, lee)—A Korean phrase that means "quick quick."

peninsula (puh-NIN-soo-luh)—A piece of land surrounded on three sides by water.

Seollal (SHE-luhl)—The Korean New Year.

taekwondo (tie-kwan-DOH)—A Korean martial art that includes kicking and punching through concentrated and precise movements.

yutnori (yah-NOO-ree)—A board game that is especially popular on the Korean New Year.

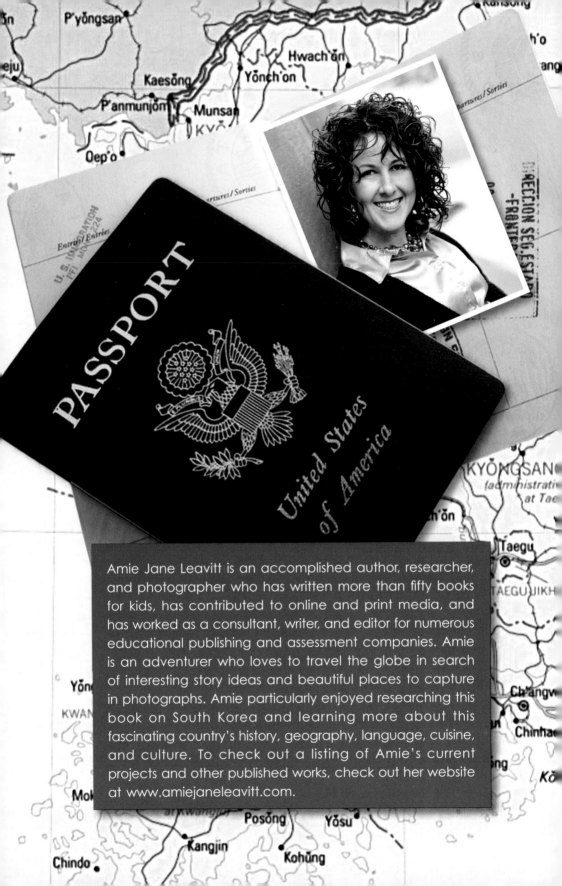

Amie Jane Leavitt is an accomplished author, researcher, and photographer who has written more than fifty books for kids, has contributed to online and print media, and has worked as a consultant, writer, and editor for numerous educational publishing and assessment companies. Amie is an adventurer who loves to travel the globe in search of interesting story ideas and beautiful places to capture in photographs. Amie particularly enjoyed researching this book on South Korea and learning more about this fascinating country's history, geography, language, cuisine, and culture. To check out a listing of Amie's current projects and other published works, check out her website at www.amiejaneleavitt.com.